THE TIMEWARP TRIALS

HENRY VIII
GUILTY OR INNOCENT?

Stewart Ross
illustrated by Élisabeth Eudes-Pascal

Defendant

DOCK

Judge,
the Honourable
Ms Winifred Wigmore

CLERK
Mr George S. Cribble

Prosecuting lawyer,
Miss Tankia Bessant

PUBLIC GALLERY/PRESS

THE
TIMEWARP
TRIALS

HENRY VIII
GUILTY OR INNOCENT?

Stewart Ross

illustrated by Élisabeth Eudes-Pascal

This book is dedicated to Thomas Ockmore, Raymond Sawyer, Phoebe Newby, Emma-Leigh Newby and the Year 6 pupils of Pitsea Junior School who helped create it.

Published in 2010 by Evans Brothers Ltd
2A Portman Mansions
Chiltern Street
London WIU 6NR

British Library Cataloguing in Publication Data

Ross, Stewart.
    Henry VIII. -- (The Timewarp Trials)
    1. Henry VIII, King of England, 1491-1547--Juvenile
    fiction. 2. Great Britain--Kings and rulers--Juvenile
    fiction. 3. Great Britain--History--Henry VIII,
    1509-1547--Juvenile fiction. 4. Trials--Juvenile fiction.
    5. Historical fiction. 6. Children's stories.
    I. Title II. Series
    823.9'14-dc22

ISBN-13: 9780237542481

Editor: Bryony Jones
Designer: D.R. Ink
Printed in Spain

The High Court of History

Witness

WITNESS BOX

Defence lawyer,
Mr Leroy Williams

JURY

In the beginning…

IT WAS PROFESSOR GEEKMEISTER'S IDEA. He said it came to him while he was watching the film *Jurassic Park* with his grandson, Charlie. If it was possible to bring a dinosaur back to life from a scrap of DNA, why couldn't it be done with a person? Maybe a famous person, someone like....

Horatio Geekmeister set to work that very evening. Shut away in his private laboratory for weeks at a time, he twiddled and fiddled and scribbled for almost two years. Finally, one wet Saturday afternoon, he cracked it. He immediately picked up his phone and called his friend, the well-known historian Doctor David Gibbon.

After explaining what he had done, the professor asked in a voice squeaking with excitement, 'So who do you think it should be, David?'

Doc David paused. 'Hmm. Well, someone well-known, I suppose.'

'Of course,' replied Geekmeister, slightly irritated. 'But who?'

'Depends what you want to do with him – or her. Do you want to keep them in the house, Horatio, all to yourself? Your own pet hero. Or do you want to put them on public display, in a glass case or something? Like a sort of historical zoo, although that might be a bit unkind.'

Geekmeister had stopped listening. 'I want,' he said very slowly, 'I want to put them on trial.'

'What?'

'You heard. I want them tried for the crimes people say they committed during their lifetime. Their first lifetime, that is. I want to find out whether they really are guilty or not.'

'Put them on trial? You mean in a court?' spluttered David.

'Precisely, my dear David. They will go on trial in a court of history that I will set up. So, who will it be?'

Doc David let out a low whistle. 'Well, in that case there's only one choice.'

'And that is?'

'Henry. King Henry VIII of England.'

'And the charge against him?'

'Easy. Not doing his job properly. Being selfish and unnecessarily cruel. Allowing his—'

Geekmeister interrupted. 'Yes, yes. But in short?'

'In short, Horatio, you can put King Henry VIII on trial for being a tyrant!'

And Horatio Geekmeister did precisely that.

He did not tell anyone where he had found his sample of Henry's DNA, but it was genuine alright. Doc David thought it might have come from one of the king's shirts that had been found in an old chest at Hampton Court. In Geekmeister's skilful hands the cells grew rapidly into a fully grown, rather grumpy middle-aged man with a red beard. Not long after that the High Court of History met and prepared to hear its first case.

The Accused

'SILENCE! SILENCE IN COURT!' barked Victor Vanwall, sergeant to the High Court.

As the muttering gradually faded away, all heads turned towards the judge. The Honourable Ms Winifred Wigmore was not one to stand for any nonsense. She glared around with icy blue eyes, daring anyone to challenge her.

'Right,' she began, 'now we have a little order here, you may bring in the accused.'

This was the moment the whole world had been waiting for: the first public appearance for almost 500 years of one of the most famous figures in all history. Heavy footsteps could be heard echoing down the long passageway that led to the courtroom. They grew louder and louder, heavier and heavier. In the public gallery necks craned, eyes stared, fingers tensed.

At last, just when the suspense had become unbearable, he appeared. Into the court strode a tall, red-bearded, square man dripping with jewels and decked out in magnificent clothing – Professor Geekmeister had taken great care to dress his creation properly. Even Judge Wigmore was impressed. But only for a moment.

Standing legs astride in the middle of the room, the man stared about him scornfully.

'So it's true then,' he began, speaking with a strange accent. 'You have brought us back to make a fool of us. Well, we'll have none of it!'

With these words, King Henry – for it really was him – lunged back towards the door. Immediately two hefty security men grabbed him and hauled him back across the room.

'Scum! Traitors! Unhand us!' roared the king as he was shoved into the dock and the low door shut and bolted from the outside. In case he thought about jumping out, one of the guards stood, arms folded, just a metre away. Swaying like a caged bear, Henry sat there sweating and scowling at the judge.

The Honourable Ms Winifred Wigmore perched gold-rimmed glasses on her pointed nose and glanced over the papers before her.

'You are Henry Tudor, sometime king of England?' she began, peering at the accused over the top of her lenses.

'No.'

'Really? Then who are you?'

'We are His Majesty Henry VIII, King of England, Ireland, France—'

'Yes, yes, we can cut out the waffle,' interrupted the judge. 'Henry Tudor, you are accused of being a selfish bully, interested only in himself and not in his people. How do you plead?'

'Plead?'

'Are you guilty or not guilty?' the judge snapped. The defendant was clearly beginning to annoy her.

Henry laughed. 'What an idiotic question!'

Judge Wigmore leaned forward and cleared her throat. 'Mr Tudor, if you do not behave, you will be returned to the place you have come from. You remember where that was?'

'Of course!'

'Where was it?'

Henry looked sheepishly down at his hands. 'Our tomb.'

'Yes, your tomb. Now, how do you plead?'

'Not guilty!'

And so began the trial of King Henry VIII.

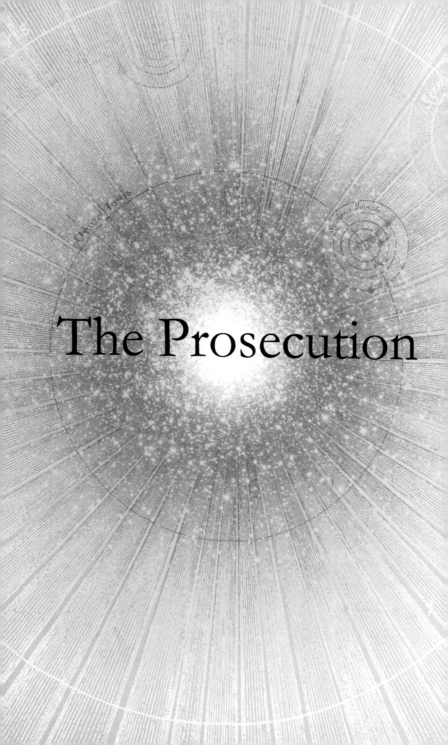

The Prosecution

AS WITH ALL TRIALS, HENRY VIII'S began with the prosecution. This was where Tankia Bessant, the prosecuting lawyer, came in. It was her job to prove that Henry was guilty. To do this she had to convince the 12-person jury sitting opposite her that Henry VIII was guilty of being a tyrant – a cruel and selfish ruler who cared more for himself than for his subjects.

Professor Geekmeister had insisted on a very special jury. Beside the four men and four women sat four children, all of whom had permission to be absent from school. Young people, the professor believed, were better judges of character than adults – and the two boys and two girls chosen to sit on the jury of the High Court of History certainly looked pretty sharp.

In the front row sat Tom Walker, a mischievous-looking boy with glasses, beside the curly-haired Jasmine Dessai. The details of the other two children, who were partly hidden behind Tom and Jasmine, were less clear.

Hmm, thought Tankia Bessant as she cast a bright eye over the dozen faces in the jury box, they shouldn't be too difficult to win over. As long as I can get the kids on my side… With a toss of her glossy black hair, she stood up and walked slowly across the court. All eyes followed her.

Standing like a headteacher before a school assembly, Miss Bessant took a deep breath and began her speech. 'Ladies and gentlemen – and children – of the jury, I would like you to look beyond me to the dock.'

The jury did as they were told.

'What do you see there?'

Tom wondered whether he should reply and turned to look at Jasmine. As he did so, the lawyer answered her own question. 'A selfish monster!' she cried. 'A beast! A man so swollen with pride and vanity and cruelty that his last wife, Catherine Parr, was delighted when he died.'

The lawyer turned towards the dock and smiled. 'Yes, Mr Tudor. Queen Catherine found a dashing young boyfriend before you were hardly in your grave. She married him a few months later.'

Gripping the wooden bar in front of him, Henry glared furiously back at his accuser. 'In another time, witch, we'd have cut off your head!' he muttered under his breath. 'Or worse!'

Luckily for Henry, Judge Wigmore did not catch what he said. Miss Bessant had heard but she said nothing. Instead, she gave Henry a look more eloquent than a thousand words. 'Just you wait, monster!' it said. 'Just you wait!'

The accused man met her gaze and let out a little laugh of scorn. The battle was on.

Tankia Bessant's case was simple. King Henry VIII, she said, was guilty of three unforgivable things.

First, he was lazy: he left important work to other people and, when they didn't do what he wanted, he simply got rid of them. Sometimes most brutally.

Second, he was greedy for money and glory. He took over the church, stole its wealth, and wasted his fortune on wars that did his country no good at all.

Third, he was horribly cruel to those he should have been most kind to, his family.

'In short,' said Prosecutor Bessant, 'you ruled England like a monster; or, more accurately, you were a dreadful, selfish king.'

Over in the dock, Henry made quite a good impression of having been so bored by the prosecutor's speech that he had fallen asleep. Ignoring his rumbling snores, Bessant turned to the jury. 'Now, respected members of the community, I will prove my case by giving you hard evidence – facts – and by calling one witness from the past to back up what I have to say. Unfortunately Professor Geekmeister has had time to bring back only one witness for me, but I tell you that if he had had more time we could have hundreds – no, thousands – who would be happy to swear that this man before you was indeed a wicked tyrant.'

As Henry's buffalo snores were still grumbling round the room, Judge Wigmore ordered Victor Vanwall, the court sergeant, to wake him so the case could continue. Although Victor was a beefy fellow, it took all his strength to persuade the defendant to open his eyes and pay attention.

'Oh!' he yawned, pretending rather badly to have just woken up. 'And we were having such a pleasant dream.' He waved a hand towards Tankia Bessant. 'In it that woman over there was having her head cut off. For lying!'

Once again the hook-nosed prosecutor ignored Henry's taunting and went on with her job. As king, she explained, Henry had spent most of his time, especially as a young man, enjoying himself. He danced, he feasted, he played and listened to music, he jousted in

tournaments, he chased deer and pretty girls…
and spent precious little time on matters
of government.

'True or not true, Mr Tudor?' Miss Bessant
demanded, spinning round to face the dock.

A broad smile spread across Henry's bearded
face. 'True, of course! Only a fool would choose
to work when they could be having fun. Anyway,
we had many skilful servants to take care of
everyday things.'

'Indeed. I was coming to that,' replied Miss
Bessant with a nod. She explained to the jury
that Henry had been served most loyally by men
like Thomas Wolsey and Thomas Cromwell.
And how had he rewarded them? Wolsey was
saved from being beheaded only by dying when
the king was about to accuse him of treason.
Cromwell was less lucky. Having provided His
Majesty with a fourth wife who was not to
the royal taste, on 28th July 1540 Mr Secretary
Cromwell had his head chopped off.

'With all the work it had to do, the royal
axe must have been pretty blunt by the end of
your bloody reign, Mr Tudor,' the prosecutor
concluded with a wry smile.

'Sharp enough for one more head,' Henry muttered into his beard.

The king's whiskers might have prevented his words reaching adult ears, but they were picked up easily enough by the children on the jury. 'He really is a monster, isn't he?' whispered Tom, leaning over towards Jasmine.

The girl shook her head. 'No way!' she said, shielding her mouth with her hand. 'He's quite cute, really.'

Before the boy could reply, Cribble the clerk brought the conversation to a halt with a quiet but meaningful cough.

Tankia Bessant spent the next half an hour telling the jury how, at the start of Henry's reign, the Pope was in charge of the Christian church in England. But, when Pope Clement VII would not let Henry get divorced, the king made himself head of the church and got his divorce that way.

Those who disagreed were executed – 'of course,' added the prosecutor with a sneer. Casting a look in the defendant's direction, she raised her neatly plucked eyebrows in scorn.

Next, using his new power, Henry had closed down all the monasteries and taken their vast treasure and lands for himself.

'What could be greedier than that?' she demanded. Much of this new wealth he wasted on wars in Ireland, Scotland and France. He made no great conquests and left only a trail of suffering and misery.

While the prosecutor was explaining all
this, Henry just sat there, sometimes nodding,
sometimes shaking his head and sighing as if to
say, 'My dear woman, you just don't have a clue
what you're talking about!'

Tankia Bessant had now reached the third arm
of her argument, Henry's cruelty. The king suddenly
began taking more interest. He sat up straight and
leaned forward to catch her every word.

'My argument is this,' she explained, standing
before the jury and passing her eye slowly over

each member in turn. 'My argument is that although Mr Tudor's behaviour was cruel and selfish in almost everything he did, he was at his cruellest towards those he should have been most kind to. His own family.'

One juryman, a round-faced man with neat curly hair, was so carried away by Miss Bessant's words that he cried out, 'Here, here!' without quite realising what he was doing.

Judge Wigmore was not impressed. 'Silence!' she ordered. 'Who was that who dared to interrupt my court?'

The round-faced man turned scarlet and gingerly raised a hand.

'You?'

'Yes, er, My Lady.'

'What in the name of Jarndice did you think you were doing?'

'Um, nothing, My Lady.'

'Nothing? Well don't do it again. If you do, I shall have you thrown out and the whole business will have to start all over again.'

Henry let out a loud groan.

'And you be quiet, too,' snapped the judge. 'You've had your warning, so be careful.'

Holding her papers before her, Prosecutor Bessant said crisply, 'Thank you, My Lady. With your permission, I would now like to call my witness.'

'Very well, Miss Bessant.'

Queen Catherine

THE PROSECUTOR GLANCED down at her notes and paused. It was a dramatic pause, done for effect and not because she was thinking what to say. She had known for a long time what name she would call. No one else in that hot, excited courtroom knew, especially not King Henry. But there was one name everyone had been hoping for. The lawyers, the clerk, the sergeant, the jury, the spectators crowded onto the benches at the back of the room, the journalists with their pads and pencils, even the judge herself... everyone now sat up a bit straighter, waiting for the words to fall from Miss Bessant's lips.

Slowly, very slowly, she raised her eyes and turned towards the clerk, Mr George S. Cribble.

'Mr Cribble, kindly call Her Majesty Queen Catherine of Aragon!'

No sooner had the words left Miss Bessant's mouth than a buzz of conversation ran around the court. 'Yes! Always wanted to know what she looked like,' said Jasmine. 'One of my heroes.'

'Oh yes?' grinned Tom. 'Strange choice. Anyway, I bet we'll get some fireworks.'

Before Jasmine could explain that Catherine was her hero because she had been so brave when Henry abandoned her, Victor Vanwell once again called for quiet.

'Si-len-ce in court!' he barked, glaring across at the jury as well as the men and women in the gallery. 'Silence – in – court!'

As the voices died away, the children became aware of another noise. It sounded like a kettle coming slowly to the boil, a sort of gentle fizzing and slow bubbling. It was Henry. He had gone bright red and was shaking as if the courtroom had been suddenly caught in an earthquake. The volcano finally exploded.

'She? A queen?!' he hissed, sounding like a giant cobra about to strike.

'Yes, you did hear correctly,' explained Miss Bessant, unnecessarily.

'Quee—'

Before he could finish, Judge Wigmore stepped in yet again. 'Get a grip on yourself, Mr Tudor. Miss Bessant can use whatever names she wishes, and I have warned you several times already about your behaviour. If you continue in this manner…'

'Alright,' sighed Henry, subsiding into his chair. 'Go on, bully us some more, Miss Bessant.'

Judge Wigmore raised an eyebrow before turning to Miss Bessant. 'You may proceed, Prosecutor. I believe you have called your first witness?'

'I have, My Lady.' She pointed towards the door on her right. 'And she is already here.'

The many heads of those in the courtroom swivelled in the direction indicated by the prosecutor's elegant forefinger. There, framed in the doorway, stood a small, plump woman in a long dress, elegant green in colour and finished at the cuffs and collar with white lace. The sleeves and bodice shimmered with jewels. On her head she wore a sort of bonnet, also green, that partly covered her greying hair. A warm, oval face of olive complexion framed sad but determined eyes.

'Kindly step into the witness box, Your Majesty.' Miss Bessant sounded a different person. No one had ever heard her so polite before.

Catherine smiled, and with short, quick steps made her way into the box. Across the court, Henry glared at her furiously.

'Your name is Catherine?' Miss Bessant asked gently.

'It is.'

'And on 11th June 1509 you were married to that man over there, King Henry VIII?'

'I was.'

'And how did he treat you?'

'Very well – at first. He said every day that he loved me.'

Miss Bessant raised a hand. 'Excuse me, but did he ever say, in those early days, that your marriage was not a true one?'

'No, not once.'

As the questioning continued, Henry became more and more agitated. Several times he looked as if he might interrupt but, remembering the judge's warning, he bit his lip and kept quiet.

Slowly, step by step, Catherine explained how over the years her husband had changed. 'We were so happy at first,' she explained. When her first son was born, on New Year's Day 1511, Henry hardly stopped dancing.

'He told me,' she said with a sad smile, 'that I was the cleverest, most beautiful queen in all Christendom.'

A shadow fell over Catherine's face. 'But the boy died just a few weeks later. We had called him "Henry" – our little Henry – and after his death my husband was never quite the same again. I was pregnant many times but only one of my babies lived. She was my daughter Mary.'

Catherine turned and for the first time looked straight at Henry. He tried to smile but it didn't quite work and ended up as an awkward grin that made him look rather silly.

'You see how he does not like to remember little Mary?' Catherine continued. 'Well, it shows he had a conscience, I suppose.'

'You think so?' interrupted Miss Bessant, who been dramatically wiping away a tear without spoiling her mascara. 'You think he really cared?'

Catherine raised a chubby finger to her chin. 'I don't know. He meant it when he said he loved me. I'm sure. And he meant it when he said he loved the next one, that Boleyn woman…'

'And the girlfriends in between? Bessie Blount, Lizzie Fitzwalter, Mary Boleyn – he loved all of them too?'

'Who knows? I don't think he knew, either. He was like a child. A great big hairy baby. One could almost feel sorry for him—'

'If he had not been so cruel,' finished Miss Bessant quickly. Catherine nodded.

Between them, with question and answer, the prosecutor and the queen then ran through Henry's family life. They talked of how

Catherine had been cast aside in favour of Anne Boleyn and how Mary, after a happy childhood, was banned from ever seeing her mother again.

The list went on and on: the execution of Anne Boleyn on false charges, the sad marriage to Anne of Cleves and the even sadder one of the 49-year-old king to the teenage Catherine Howard, which was also finished with the axe. The young Elizabeth branded illegitimate when her mother, Anne Boleyn, was beheaded, and Catherine of Aragon herself…

'How did you end your days, Your Majesty?' asked Miss Bessant kindly.

'Almost alone, in one room of an old, cold castle miles from anywhere. Kimbolton I think the place was called. Most people were too frightened to come to see me. I was dying of cancer, too. Cancer of the heart.'

On hearing this, the court fell silent for a few moments. Jasmine and Tom felt deeply uncomfortable. The only movement came from Henry, who sat in the dock playing an imaginary violin.

'And when he heard of your death,' Miss Bessant added, 'it is said that he celebrated with music and dancing.'

Catherine made no reply.

With that, Miss Bessant's case for the prosecution was almost over. She summed up everything that had been said, before uttering these final words:

'So, ladies, gentlemen and children of the jury, surely there can now be no room for doubt? No room whatsoever. That man there, that beast, that monster was not fit to live, let alone rule as a king. All he touched turned to misery, blood and tears. There is only one verdict for you to give.

Of being a tyrant, a selfish bully, interested only in himself and not in his people, Henry VIII is guilty!'

Leaving those words ringing in the jury's ears, Miss Bessant nodded to the judge and sat down. Over in the dock, Henry looked decidedly uncomfortable.

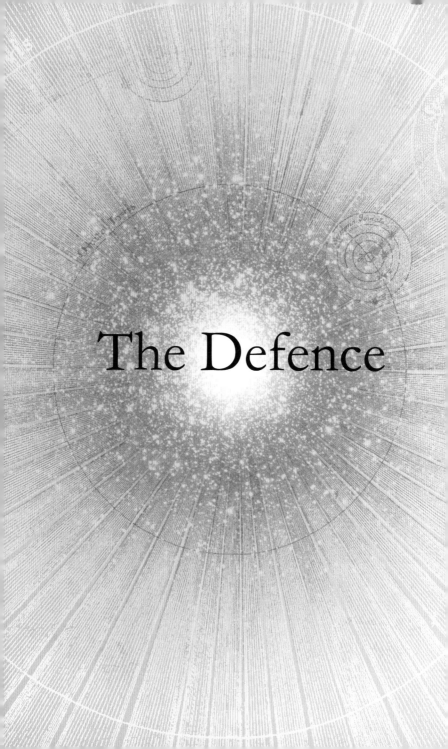

The Defence

IF IT WERE POSSIBLE to imagine the complete opposite of Prosecutor Bessant, then defence lawyer Leroy Williams was just such a person. He was relaxed, easy-going, friendly and charming. Where Miss Bessant terrified juries, he wooed them; where she bamboozled, he explained; where she grew cross, he simply smiled; where she spoke with passion, he answered with sweet reason.

'My Lady,' he began when the Honourable Ms Winifred Wigmore called on him to defend Henry VIII against Miss Bessant's accusations. 'My Lady, I thank you.'

With a broad smile on his lips, Leroy Williams turned to face the jury. 'Dear me!' he began, shaking his head. 'Dear, dear me! What a bellyful of fire has my learned friend Miss Bessant unloaded upon you. I'm surprised you're not burned to cinders by now.'

Grinning broadly, Jasmine wrote, 'I like him!!!' on a slip of paper and passed it across to Tom. He nodded vigorously.

Williams glanced over his shoulder at Henry, who was leaning forward anxiously. 'Can anyone really be as evil as that man has been painted? Do you really believe he is a devil, a monster, as

Miss Bessant would have you believe? I think not. No, my dear jury members, I think not. Indeed, I am sure not. And I will prove it to you. All you have to do is sit back, relax and listen to my story.'

That said, the defence lawyer moved casually over to stand before the dock. 'Good afternoon, Your Majesty.'

Henry, not quite sure what to make of this sudden change of tone, nodded majestically.

'You have heard, sire, all that has been said against you?'

'We have, Mr, er – how do they call you, Mr Lawyer Fellow?'

'My name, sire, is Leroy Williams.'

'We thought so. "Le roy" – that's French for "the king"! Bless my soul! So you are a king, too!'

The defence lawyer grinned. 'Well, not quite like yourself, sire. Shall we say I am a king in a different kind of court, the law court?'

'Very good!' roared Henry, who had fully recovered his spirits after Miss Bessant's battering. 'We shall get along famously—'

The voice of the judge cut him short. 'Yes, yes, all very nice, Mr Williams. But you are supposed to be defending this man, not asking him to be best man at your wedding. Now get on with it, sir!'

'Yes, My Lady. I apologise for the delay.'

After glancing down at his papers, the lawyer began to speak as he moved back towards the jury. 'The most important thing to remember,' he explained, 'is what things were like when the accused man was first alive. Did he live in our times, or even in the times of our parents or our grandparents? No, my friends, he lived 500 years ago. Life was not the same—'

By this time Henry was so excited he couldn't help interrupting. 'Well said, Mr Leroy! Of course it was not the same. We had proper kings – and queens – then. People of action, not just puppets to speak at ceremonies…'

Mr Williams held up his hands in dismay. 'Yes, sire! We know, sire. But this is not quite the right time or place for such things. If you would be so good as to let me continue…?'

Henry nodded graciously and the lawyer went on with the defence. One could not judge the king by our standards, he said. It would, of course, be quite wrong to cut off the head of a queen – or anyone else – in the 21st century. But not in Tudor times. Executions, torture, branding, flogging and all kinds of other nasty goings on were quite normal. In fact, beheading was thought the kindest way of ending someone's life. As long as the axeman aimed straight, it was much less painful than being strung up on the end of a rope or burned alive or pulled to pieces on a rack.

'Indeed,' Leroy Williams exclaimed, waving his arms about in excitement, 'would you say that Henry VIII's behaviour was any worse than that of his elder daughter?'

He turned to the jury. 'I am talking, my friends, about Mary, the only child of His Majesty and Queen Catherine, the lady everyone so admired just now. When she became queen, Mary had 300 of her own wretched subjects burned to death just because they did not have the same religious faith as herself. I repeat, burned to death! Imagine it! The flames licking at your feet…'

Jasmine pulled a face and covered her ears. Just talk of gory things made her feel sick. Even Tom, who thought he liked bloodthirsty stories, was a bit flustered. He tried to imagine how human flesh would burn… Yuk!

Judge Wigmore had noticed the girl's reaction and interrupted sharply. 'Really, Mr Williams! This is not a horror show. Spare us the gruesome details.'

'Yes. I apologise, My Lady. I was simply making the point that Henry lived in cruel times, when people thought and behaved differently from ourselves. We cannot condemn him simply because he was not like us.'

Leroy Williams turned to the dock. 'Is that correct, Your Majesty?'

Henry beamed. 'Perfectly, Mr Leroy. Couldn't have put it better myself.'

'Thank you, sire.'

The defence lawyer moved on to his second point. Much of what Henry did was for the sake of England, not just himself. Again, Mr Williams turned to the dock.

'Your Majesty, would you be kind enough to tell the court why you divorced your first wife?'

Henry frowned. 'No, Mr Leroy.'

'I beg your pardon?'

'No, I will not tell this court or anyone else why I divorced Queen Catherine, because I did not divorce her. We were never married. She had been married to my elder brother, Arthur, and it is against God's law to marry a lady who has previously been married to your brother.'

'Yet…'

'Yes, I know, Mr Leroy. I was tricked by Pope Julius II – Bishop of Rome – into believing it was alright to marry Catherine. God showed me the truth by not giving us any sons. Simple as that.'

'Perhaps,' smiled Leroy Williams. 'And when Pope Clement VII refused to see the mistake Pope Julius had made, you broke away from the Roman Catholic Church?'

'I had no choice. For England's sake I had to have a son to carry on after me, and I hoped Anne Boleyn would give me that son.'

'Why were you so keen to have a son, sire?'

'Really, Mr Leroy! Don't you know your history? My father battled his way to the crown after years of bloody warfare. The "Wars of the Roses" they call them now, when the red rose of Lancaster fought against the white rose of York. My father was of the House of Lancaster, my mother from the House of York. We, the Tudors, brought peace. Our badge was the red and white rose united. If I failed to provide a son to take over after me, the roses might fall apart again.

'Think of it, Mr Leroy. More war, more pain, more misery. Was I wrong to try to prevent that?

I had to be firm, harsh even – but only to stop something far, far worse from happening.'

Henry sat down and, taking a large red and white handkerchief from his sleeve, began mopping his brow.

Leroy Williams paused for the king's words to sink in before addressing the jury. 'There you have it, my friends. The defendant might not have been a kindly king, but he did his duty. He did what was right for his country – and that is

what all kings are supposed to do. That shows he
cared about his people.'

Tom picked up his pencil and wrote,
'Difficult, isn't it?' on the paper Jasmine had
used. She glanced across at what he had written
and mouthed, 'Very!'

The lawyer was now standing before the
judge. 'At this point, My Lady,' he announced,
'I will, with your permission, end the case
for the defence by calling my witness,
Mr Thomas Cromwell.'

Cromwell

'EH?' JASMINE HEARD one of the children behind her whisper. 'Who's he?' She wanted to turn round and explain but thought better of it. Her new friend and jury-mate would find out soon enough.

Thomas Cromwell was a most surprising choice of witness. At first his pasty face, long nose and small, darting eyes did not appeal to the jury. One or two of them could be seen frowning as he made his way into the witness box with tidy steps.

But Leroy Williams had chosen carefully and cleverly. 'You know why you are here, Mr Cromwell?' he began.

'I do.'

The lawyer pointed to the dock. 'And you recognise that man over there?'

'I do.'

'You were his chief minister for many years, I believe?'

'I was, yes.'

'And what happened in the end?'

'The end?'

'I mean when you were no longer chief minister.'

'I was executed. My head was severed from my body on 28th July 1540.'

Tom stared hard, looking for a scar on the man's neck. Nothing was visible.

'In case you're wondering, I didn't feel a thing,' added Cromwell with a hint of a smile.

'I'm glad to hear it, Mr Cromwell. Would you mind if I now ask the defendant a few questions?'

'Please do.'

Turning to King Henry, the lawyer was surprised to find the defendant looking extremely sad, almost in tears. 'Your Majesty,' he asked, 'was Mr Cromwell a loyal and able servant of yours?'

The king sniffed. 'Oh! He was, he was! Yes indeed. The best I ever had. Clever, hard-working…'

'Yes, thank you. So why on earth did you agree to his being beheaded?'

The king banged his fist against the wooden rail in front of him. 'I was a fool, Mr Leroy. A fool! I listened to the Duke of Norfolk's lies about Mr Cromwell and, because I was cross at the time, I believed them. Cromwell had made a mistake, of course. He had arranged for me to marry some horse-faced woman from Germany.'

Leroy Williams turned back to the witness box. 'Is this true, Mr Cromwell?'

'It is.'

'And your execution was more the fault of the Duke of Norfolk than the king?'

'I suppose it was.'

'So you don't blame His Majesty for what happened to you?'

Cromwell looked shocked. 'Blame him? No, not at all. He was the king. I was ambitious. I was playing a dangerous game and I knew what would happen if I failed.'

'Then you would not describe King Henry as a selfish monster, even though he was responsible for your death?'

Cromwell raised an eyebrow in surprise. 'A monster? He was difficult, up and down in his moods, always falling for pretty girls…'

The king jumped to his feet. 'Treason! Enough of that, Cromwell!'

The judge tapped her pencil on the desk in front of her. 'Now, now, Mr Tudor. Remember what we said…'

Henry subsided and Cromwell continued as if nothing had happened. 'Yes, he was always falling for pretty girls and, like everyone who has been spoilt all their life, he liked to have his own way. He got much worse as he grew older. But he was no monster. He had too much respect for the law, his duty and his God.'

Leroy Williams nodded. 'Thank you, Mr Cromwell. That will be all.'

Thomas Cromwell bowed his head slightly and walked from the court as neatly as he had entered it. When he had gone, the defence lawyer turned back to the jury. 'There you have it, my friends: even a man who had been executed by Henry VIII agrees that the king did his duty by his people.'

He looked towards the dock. 'I am not saying that the man sitting before you was a good king,' he went on, staring hard at Henry. 'I am not even saying that he was a good man. Indeed, one might even say that he was a rather unpleasant fellow.'

Henry opened his mouth to speak but Williams shook his head. 'Not now, Your Majesty,' he said firmly. 'No, my friends, we are not here to judge His Majesty's character but his kingship.'

Leroy Williams had now planted himself squarely in the centre of the court. 'Henry did what he believed was best for England. His Majesty was England's majesty. He established the country's Royal Navy, he gave it its own church, he defended it with a string of castles along the southern coast, he saw that the government worked as well as any in Europe at that time. He respected the law.

Was Thomas Cromwell executed just because the king ordered it, as a monster might have done? No. He was executed by an Act of Parliament. By the law of the land.

This was not the way of a bad king. My friends on the jury, if you find this man guilty of being a tyrant, you will be doing a great injustice. King Henry VIII, one of our most memorable monarchs, served his country excellently. In a word, he is quite clearly not guilty of the charges against him!'

Henry sprang to his feet, let out a whoop of delight and started clapping furiously. 'In-no-cent! In-no-cent!' he boomed. After a minute or so, however, when he realised no one was joining in, he looked around sheepishly and sat down again.

'Wally?' wrote Jasmine. Tom shrugged and scribbled 'Tricky' on the pad before him. Jasmine smiled in agreement.

Standing with his hands clasped before him, Leroy Williams had ignored the royal pantomime. When it was over, he nodded

politely towards the judge – 'That will be all, My Lady' – and sat down. Immediately a buzz of conversation started up around the court.

Sergeant Vanwall sprang to his feet for a third time. 'Silence!'

When all was quiet, Judge Wigmore glanced down at the notes she had been making then turned to address the jury. 'Representatives of the community, you have a very important decision to make. A very important one indeed.

Miss Bessant has explained to you why she believes the man in the dock, Mr Henry Tudor, ruled England as a dreadful, selfish monster. You may or may not agree with her.

You have also heard Mr Williams saying that Mr Tudor was nothing of the sort. You must now decide whether Mr Tudor, also known as King Henry VIII, is guilty or not. If guilty, he will spend the rest of his second life behind bars. If you find him not guilty, he will be free to follow a normal life.

The decision is yours. I would now ask you to retire from the court to reach your verdict.'

Dear Reader,

YOU are a member of the jury! You were one of the two children sitting behind Jasmine and Tom. Perhaps you were the one who had not heard of Thomas Cromwell?

Go to www.evansbooks.co.uk/TimeWarpTrials and record your decision: Henry VIII, guilty or not guilty of being a selfish bully, interested only in himself and not in his people?

You will then be able to see how others have voted.

Henry VIII

1491	Born to King Henry VII and Elizabeth of York.
1494	Made Duke of York.
1502	Elder brother Arthur, married to Catherine of Aragon, dies.
1509	Henry VII dies. Henry becomes king. Marries Catherine of Aragon.
1512	War against France (to 1513).
1516	Princess Mary born.
1527	In love with Anne Boleyn, tries to separate from Catherine of Aragon.
1532	Recognised as 'Supreme Head of the English Church' by Catholic bishops.
1533	Marries Anne Boleyn. Princess Elizabeth born.

1491

1533

1509

1536   Anne Boleyn executed.
        Marries Jane Seymour.
        Begins to seize the monasteries
        Major rebellion against Henry,
        the 'Pilgrimage of Grace'.
1537   Prince Edward born.
        Jane Seymour dies.
1540   Marries and divorces Anne of Cleves.
        Marries Catherine Howard.
        Thomas Cromwell executed.
1542   Catherine Howard executed.
        Fighting with Scotland (to end of reign).
1543   Marries Catherine Parr.
        War with France (to 1546).
1547   Dies.

1543

1547

1540